small ghost

trista mateer

Trigger warnings: depression, mental health issues, mental illness, suicidal ideation, among others.

Published by Central Avenue Publishing, an imprint of Central Avenue Marketing Ltd.
www.centralavenuepublishing.com

SMALL GHOST

978-1-77168-386-9 (pbk)
978-1-77168-387-6 (ebk)

Published in Canada

Printed in United States of America

1. POETRY / Women Authors   2. POETRY / Subject & Themes - Motivational

1 3 5 7 9 10 8 6 4 2

*For anyone who feels like
pulling the sheets over their head instead of
getting out of bed in the morning.*

And for you.

You belong here.

small ghost

small ghost haunts her own apartment

It is hers and it isn't hers.
"Roommate" is a strange word for the way he moved in
and rearranged all of her furniture
without her permission.
She doesn't remember asking him to be here,
but there are a lot of things she doesn't remember doing.
She doesn't remember running straight into her
grandmother's birdbath when she was a child either,
but she has the scar to prove it.
Well, she had the scar to prove it,

but she misplaced it with the rest of her skin somewhere.

It's strange,
all the things you forget about
when you can't find the scars to prove they happened
anymore.

small ghost rattles chains in the hall

brings up the past more than anyone ever should /

stands staring off into space /

fills the tub until it runs over /

chides herself for being wasteful /

taps the lighter on the table three times for good luck /

wants to drown herself out /

tries to hang herself dry /

makes lists of things she's never going to do /

Low, fragile, inconsolable, pathetically blue.

She doesn't talk to anybody.
She goes around weeping, frightening the neighbors,
losing her mind a little over every inconvenience.

[gripping the bathroom sink] What the hell is going on?
It's always something.

It was fine for a while, but now
everything is
piling
up.

Dust.

Mail.

Atrocities.

She overthinks   everything   she does in front of people.

She fears judgment,   so she's stuck between worlds.

It would take too much effort to fix everything,
so why bother trying?

                    It's so hard to find purpose.

small ghost communicates with the living

Or, she tries to.

She bangs the pots and pans together.
She dumps the laundry on the floor.
She lights every candle in the house.
She just wants someone to look at her again.

small ghost goes grocery shopping

Well, she's not shopping.
Well, she doesn't think she's shopping.

She can't remember why she's here.

She does something close to pacing
in the fruit juice aisle,
starts crying next to the cranberry concentrate.
Doesn't remember why.

small ghost is on the edge again

About to just lose it, about to just give the game away,
about to have a total mental breakdown
any time she even thinks about telling someone
how she feels.
I mean, it's embarrassing to be so sad,
to be so weak,
to be so breakable,
and

there's no one left to talk to anyway.
She's been dead so long all her old friends have
moved on to greener pastures.
Time passing and all that.
Time devouring.
Time eating away at you and your little life.

She found a book on getting better,
couldn't even pick it up.
Hand went right through it.

small ghost will be your server tonight

Can I get you started with a drink?

She continues to show up for the night shift.
Force of habit.
She might be dead,
but she still needs to keep the lights
flickering on.

And I, of ladies most deject and wretched,

this year is one of those
dreadful ones / left out of
the memoirs / not even sad
in an interesting way /

she considers buying
some flowers and lying
in the creek out back
like Ophelia / or eating
her weight in frosting / or
scooping out her insides
with a melon baller /

most / if not all /
seems lost

small ghost spends six hours on tumblr

A day.

At least.

Looking at sad quotes,
accidentally learning Greek mythology,
getting caught up in shipping wars,
pretending to be a poet,
pretending to be a person.

There are so many lonely people
who are afraid to talk about their loneliness
outside of the internet,
like speaking the word in a coffee shop downtown
might make it too real.

She's never understood why.
Loneliness, for her, was always easy to call by its name.

small ghost sobs for sixty-five minutes

Calls it a personal best.
She keeps trying to break her own records.
She keeps crying over people who don't exist anymore
or people who don't matter anymore.

Maybe both.

She's not sad,   not really,
not over any one thing in particular.
It's just that all her sighs are heavy ones
and all the news is bad news.
It's just that she's tired of the day-to-day.
She can't do that hopeless routine one more time.

small ghost talks to strangers online

Epidemic loneliness rages on,
and even the undead are turning to the internet these days
to make friends,

to be seen without the consequences of being seen,

to be known without the consequences of being known.

She's drawn to the weirdos,
and the lovers, and the fighters,
bards, and the artists,
and of course the nail-biters,
the loners, the losers,
the tarts, and the cherries,
dreamers, and poets, and witches, and fairies.

small ghost writes a poem

In fact, she writes the same poem
over and over and over and over
until there's no paper left in your house,
until there's no surface not covered in her blood.
And then she posts it online.

It's not even a good poem.
Everyone agrees.

But still—
there's something about emptying her guts out
to people who don't ask for her name
that doesn't feel *good*,

but it feels okay.

small ghost checks her search history

spectrophobia / catoptrophobia / eisoptrophobia /
why are there three different words for fear of mirrors
/ how to make yourself feel alive again / why can't
I sleep at night / what does it mean to feel this
empty all the time / does thread count on sheets
really make a difference / is the moon hollow / is the
moon really an alien spaceship / how many calories
does anxiety burn / what do panic attacks feel like /
pixies where is my mind lyrics / how much tequila
do I need to drink to die again / spoken word poetry /
aren't I too old to still be this sad / cute dog videos

small ghost retraces her steps

Walks in circles around her problems.
Wears a path into the bedroom carpet.
Mourning noon and night,
overthinking everything that's ever happened.

Like she can go back.
Like she can change it.

The moment is over but she's stuck in it forever.

Nothing feels as shiny and new as it used to.
I'm losing track of the plot.
I'm hiding in here because I'm avoiding longing.
Living like this makes dreaming too painful to bear.
The more it hurts, the less you're able to speak about it.
I am the most negative space in the room.
I take five points of psychic damage
anytime someone mentions love.
I still believe in love devoutly.
I long for the sun but the moon always finds me instead.
Do you understand what I mean?
I often wonder if it's just bearable sadness
and everyone carries it around easily except for me.
Who could be more lost than I am?
Who could be more desperate?
What's the most upsetting part of being so useless?
You tell me.
You tell me.

small ghost gets creative

She makes things so people know she's still here.
She makes things so she knows she's still here.

Once she signed up for an origami class.

Once she pulled out all of your kitchen knives
and dropped them in your neighbor's pool.

Once she stood at the foot of your bed,
whispered poetry while you were sleeping,
and then rearranged all of your picture frames.

Once she tried to draw a self-portrait,
but she couldn't remember what she looked like.

small ghost doesn't clean her room

It's been eighty-two days since she last made her bed.
Between trash and clothes, she can't see the floor.
She slept next to a pizza box for six nights in a row.

At first it was a lack of motivation to do anything.

Now the mess just makes it easier for her to disappear.

small ghost watches *glee* on netflix

She likes the juxtaposition;

it makes her feel like a parody of herself,
like she's simultaneously supposed to be better than this
and worse than this,
>> because she's worse than bad TV
>> because she's nothing
>> because she's nothing
>> because she's nothing
>> because she's nothing
>> because she's nothing
>> because she's nothing
>> because she's nothing
>> because she's nothing
>> because she's nothing.

But it takes an awful lot of work to be nothing
sometimes,

and it only takes a medium amount of work
to cry over weird Journey covers.

small ghost plays *skyrim*

Just to listen to the tavern banter.

Just to walk around outside
somewhere with clean air
and two moons.

Just to be someone again

with a clear purpose

and enough goals

to keep moving forward.

small ghost goes on a quest

It's dangerous out there,
so first there's the armor,
high pony, and a sword or two.
She says she was a knight in a past life,
or maybe a pirate craving oranges,
or maybe a damsel because,
you know,
she's used to being in distress,
and anyway,

back to the matter at hand.

There's something she has to do
outside of the house today,
and she needs to play pretend to get it done.

What was it again?

We should get oranges.

There are too many people here.

Someone made eye contact with me.

Everyone knows I'm barely holding it together.

Oh, yes.
My throne of dirty laundry.
My kingdom of unwashed dishes.

No one is clean here, by decree.
Queen of self-medication.
Jester of making it work.
It takes sweat and tears
to become something.
Even something like this.

afraid all the time / losing interest
in almost everything / basic hygiene
feels like a chore with too many steps
/ she knows it's ridiculous / that's the
worst part / she knows it's not a big deal
/ other people manage just fine / but
she's not other people / she's something
worse / something stagnant / swamped
under the weight of her own feelings /
stuck in bed contemplating existential
questions instead of making breakfast

God I want to be left alone

Or otherwise forgotten

Burn every photo I'm in

Leave me

In the woods somewhere and

Never come back for me

small ghost collects things

Steals your Pokémon cards,
stacks your books up to the ceiling,
keeps dropping rings into your dresser drawers.

She hoards bottles of the perfume
her mother used to wear.

She breaks all the plates just to order new ones,
just to have something to look forward to
for three to seven days.

She pulls out a credit card in the middle of the night
to buy the Barbie she had when she was ten.
Tattoo Barbie.
You know, with the pink crochet bikini
and the butterflies.
And the sleepaway case too, with the fold-out bed.

Remember that?
Remember unadulterated delight?

Maybe you can catch it again.
Maybe you can find it on eBay.

elsewhere

Instead of sleeping,
I am wide awake dreaming of a different world.

In the dream, I grow old with my childhood
best friend on the same block where we met /
everything is in bloom / even us / time is passing
but it's beautiful / love lives forever and the stars
know us by name / they treat us like distant
relatives / everyone is good / everyone is redeemable /
everything is okay / I don't even need to speak
because I am already understood.

Can you really blame me for wanting to stay there?

Everything is loud.   Everything is broken.
My bad moods are evergreen, and
all the lights are too bright.

I don't know how to plan for the future
in a world like this,   so I don't.

Is this life   or just something like it?

Everywhere I turn, there's another subscription fee.
Can I be done yet? Can I log out?

        I want to fuck off into the ocean.

This can't be all there is.

And the world keeps turning;   how fucked up is that.

Bleak,   but we stay silly.

I take joy in the little things, but Jesus Christ is it hard.

I'm watching people forget me.

    Who I really was. What I was like before this.

It's not their fault.   I'm forgetting too.

small ghost binges *friends* (again)

She finds it kind of comforting
to just lie there on the couch, knowing she'll hear
someone say, *I'll be there for you*

roughly every twenty-three minutes.

It's easier than picking up the phone and asking for help.

It's easier than most things.

small ghost plays *animal crossing*

Spends hours and hours
        hours and hours
        hours and hours

rearranging an untouchable house because
she   knows

there will never be an opportunity for her
to have a real home,
to belong to a real place.

So she puts in her time,
builds all her furniture, trades for nothing,
cleans up the beaches every day,
checks in on her neighbors,
feels
        something like relief

when she realizes this virtual island
might be the last beautiful thing she ever creates.

small ghost has another breakdown

Small ghost watches the blood pump in your neck.
Small ghost fills up the bathtub just to drain it.
Small ghost wants to crawl into bed with her mother.
Small ghost is so tired.
She's so tired.
She's so fucking tired.

The cobwebs in her head feel so heavy, you know?
And it's like when they started spinning themselves
it wasn't such a big deal,
but now that they're here????
They're just so heavy.
  She's just so tired.
    She's just so . . .
      She's just . . .
She paces the kitchen,
walks past your new set of knives over and over,
has to remind herself twice in the span of five minutes,

You can't kill something that's already dead.

And isn't that the point?
Isn't that why she became a small ghost anyway?

She can't remember when she started
digging her own grave,
but now she can't stop hovering over it.

Loneliness has its mouth on me.
Loneliness has its hands all over me.
Loneliness is eating me alive,

but at least it's touching me.

I speak and words just fall right through people.
I don't know how else to explain it.

I wish   you could hear me.

I wish I had something worth saying.

Everything is always going to be too much for me.

She's ready to be stardust again.

It's not her fault.

She was made this way.

Like a cheap plastic doll
with faulty parts.

She's always going to be
a broken little girl.

Sorry for ignoring your texts
and never picking up the phone.
It's just that nothing
is worth talking about anymore.
I don't want to bore you
and I don't want to worry you
and I'm convinced
those are the only two options.
I'm embarrassed to admit
how bad it's getting again.

small ghost talks to the mirror

[transcript of disembodied voice recorded at 3 a.m.]

Sickening
how much
you need
to be liked.

So desperate
for affection
everyone
can see it
on you
like a stain.

You're obsessed
with controlling
how people
perceive you
because you know
they're going
to leave
and you think
you can stop it.

You can't.

The fig tree.   The pomegranate.
I know what I'm made of.
Dead dreams and bad spirits.
Crimes of passion   and Coke Zero.
The old prophecies all say
     I'll end up like my father.
I hate watching them come true;
I didn't intend to be here for that.

It's getting dark in here
so she pushes everyone away
and then waits
for someone to circle back
and rescue her from herself.

IT'S JUST YOU NOW.

ALL ALONE.

YOU AND YOUR THUNDER

AND YOUR FLOODS.

YOU AND YOUR BIBLICAL ANGER.

WHAT WILL YOU TURN IT ON

WHEN YOU'RE THE ONLY THING LEFT

IN THE ROOM?

the age-old cycle

sometimes she talks herself down but when that doesn't
work / she spirals and turns evil / she fights herself to
the death or burns out trying / until all that's left of her
world is ruin / and time has forsaken her

draft 9 / this feels overdramatic /
but what if nobody's happy? / aren't
you tired of doing what everyone else
wants you to do? / I'm having a problem
/ I haven't hated every minute of it / but
I've hated enough to want to quit / life
has made me angry and I want to return
the favor / I had a dream once where
I was adored / and I want to go back

Been here
a thousand times.

Halfway down
I always change my mind.

what a joke

So a ghost floats into the doctor's office
complaining of sadness and stagnancy

and the doctor says,
Have you tried living a little?

FORGIVE ME FOR NOT ADVOCATING FOR MYSELF

She's only just begun to admit she has a problem.
How is she supposed to prove to a stranger
that she needs help?

Where is the evidence of her destruction?

Where is the proof she is barely   here?

Small Ghost wishes on a star

for a car accident on the way to work,
a sinkhole opening up under the house,
a very specific meteor strike.

(Her wishes never seem to come true.)

Things will be better next year.

In January, I will breathe easier.

February will be sweeter.

I will resurrect in March.

I will live again in the spring.

By April, I'll be blooming like everything else.

In May, I'll try again—I swear it.

In June, under the sun, I'll know who I am.

Summer will take me by the hand and shake me awake.

July will bring me back to myself.

August is for starting over.

I'll rally in September.

Autumn's like a blanket for the soul.

In October, under the moon, I'll recommit to myself.

By November, I'm sure I'll be fine.

December will be lonely, but it's mine.

Crisp winter air always reminds me I'm alive.

Things will be better next year.

small ghost has been here for ages

Talking to the skeletons in the closet,
digging holes in the backyard,
floating down to CVS in her pajamas.

Time keeps passing.
Isn't that funny?
Isn't that strange?
Isn't that rude?

There were people she was supposed to be.

There were things she was supposed to do.

small ghost visits her parents

Walks the familiar path to her childhood bedroom
only to find it redecorated.

      Who lives here again?

These people don't know her.

She lies down in the attic and sleeps for a year.

small ghost leaves notes around the house

They all say things like:

THIS ISN'T RIGHT

THIS DOESN'T FEEL RIGHT

GET OUT OF HERE

LEAVE THIS PLACE

YOU'RE NOT SUPPOSED TO BE HERE

small ghost is talking to herself again

I don't belong here /

It's killing me. It's killing me. The weight of everything /

I am often difficult. I know I should be sorry for it /

They used to say I had potential, but now /

My chemicals are all confused /

Can't you see how hard it is? /

Feeling intolerable and eternal. Tired of fighting /

All this melodrama and mundane tragedy /

There are so many terrible things to be scared of and /

My head is constantly full of little horrors /

It's inescapable. It's like /

I was cursed but I don't remember who by /

small ghost wakes up at 4 a.m.

To do even this, she has to set an alarm.
Once it goes off,
she still stays in bed until the sun goes down,
likes spending her time
moving things around the house
when nobody else is awake to see her do it.

Yesterday
the thought of ending my life
filled me with relief, wrapped me up
like a heated blanket
(it kept me warm all night)

but today
I don't know—

today I threw open the curtains
and put on the news
and

everything was still bad to be honest,
even   worse than before.

small ghost runs away from her problems

Doesn't say where she's going.
Doesn't say when she's coming back.

She's sure it's going to be different there.
Fresh air.
No more haunting, just relaxing.

But when she gets to the hotel room,
she locks the door and draws the curtains closed

and checks the lock on the door

and checks the lock on the door

and checks the lock again on the door

and everything's fine.

Everything's going to be fine.

The farthest she makes it from the hotel room
is the corner store.

small ghost shares a few too-honest poems about her life

gets furious whenever
people have the nerve to ask
if she's writing about herself
/ goes scorched-earth on the
comments section / full of
strangers / trying to help her

mother says it doesn't run in the family
/ except for that one cousin no one talks
about / grandmother says we're all
perfectly normal except for her sister
who was institutionalized and her aunt
who jumped out a window and *anyway* /
why are you so obsessed with getting
diagnosed? / she says / *you're normal*
/ *you're fine* / *we're normal* / *we're fine*

small ghost moans inside the walls

And gives up on every project she starts.

She puts podcasts on when you're asleep
so you wake up scared someone's in the house.

She runs a Sharpie through all of your books
and talks shit about everyone you know.

She twists up all of your jewelry
and turns off your alarms
and no one can stop her.

No one knows how.

Not even her.

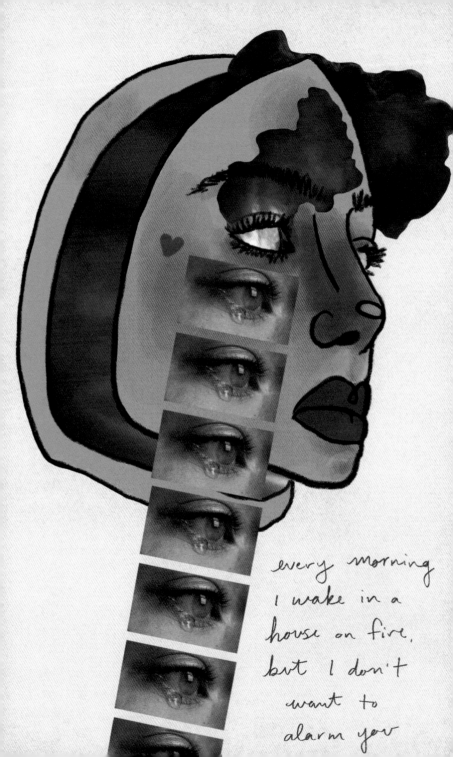

every morning
I wake in a
house on fire,
but I don't
want to
alarm you

small ghost hides in the corner

And talks to the cat
instead of making eye contact
with her family.

She floats into the bathroom
and writes on the wall:

No one is even going to remember
I was here.

Nothing around here ever changes.

There are moments of clarity
where I know everything isn't as bad as it seems.
Whole months, head above water.
But when you're drowning, you're drowning.
It doesn't matter how many months a year
you spend on land.

And I am nineteen, telling myself,
I'm going to grow out of this.
And I am twenty-five, convincing myself,
My world is not ending.
And I am thirty-two, promising myself,
It gets better.

Because it doesn't matter if it's true or not;
it's what you have to believe
in order to survive.

small ghost throws in the towel

Actually she throws out the towel.
Actually, in a fit of distress,
she throws out all of your towels.

It's hard to watch you clean up messes
when she feels like one herself.

It's hard and it's not getting less hard.
It's hard and it's not getting easier.
It's hard and it's not getting better.

How do you accept you've lost a fight
with yourself?

small ghost goes to therapy

and no /

she doesn't know how that makes her feel

*Okay. Today let's try
this one. Everyone needs
community, right?*

Everyone needs community, yeah.

*What about you? Who
do you go to when you
have a problem? Where
do you turn when you
need help?*

EVERYONE NEEDS COMMUNITY
EXCEPT FOR ME
BECAUSE IF I CAN'T HACK IT ALONE
I DESERVE TO SUFFER

What are you writing down?

& who could I trust with the catastrophe of my feelings?

How could I let someone love me?
How could I do this to another person?
Who wants to watch me rot in bed?
Who wants to watch me waste my life?
Come join me in this black hole.

It feels selfish to even think about.

Free me from my heart. Desire is a trap.

How do you stop feeling things so intensely?

(You don't.)

I remember being happy but I don't ever remember being at
ease. What if I never get better than this?

No, I'm not going to call you back.

Life for other people seems effortless,
but the walls are closing in on me.

; Oh, woe is me,

wore the same sweatpants
for three months in a row /
where does the time go? / she
thinks about her last words
twelve times a day / regret is
a thing you carry even after
death / the mania is all fun and
games until it's not / everything
she does is an attempt to avoid
having strong feelings / otherwise
it's all apocalyptic daydreams
and worst-case scenarios / she
gets into the shower and weighs
the probability of a serial killer
breaking in through the sliding
glass door / she cries thinking
about her brother dying even
though it hasn't happened /
her mother said all this worry
was normal / but it wasn't

Why am I like this? Well,

I tend to ignore all my late-night epiphanies

and I was taught to hold grudges instead of hands.

All I know about love is that it involves obsession.

Feral creatures aren't socialized properly, you know,

and what is it even like to sleep for eight hours a night?

Maybe I need to read more cliché motivational quotes.

Maybe I enjoy torturing myself and playing the victim.

Who's to say?

small ghost barely remembers her childhood

She tries to make peace with the past,
but it's never there when she goes looking.
There are flashes sometimes.
Memories that feel like they belong to someone else.

All she really remembers is wanting to grow up,
    wanting to be free,   wanting to feel safe.

[transcript of disembodied voice recorded at 3 a.m.]

But then you grow up

                    and nowhere is safe.

small ghost is starving

Like a lumbering beast waking from winter,
great maw agape.

Empty.

Empty.

Begging to be filled.
Ravenous for something she cannot bear to name.

SMALL GHOST MADE SADNESS
HER PERSONALITY

AND NOW WHAT?

NOW WHAT?   NOW WHAT?

RECOVERY IS HARDER WHEN YOU DON'T
REMEMBER WHO YOU USED TO BE.

I DON'T WANT TO HAVE TO DO THE WORK
IT WILL TAKE TO REMEMBER.

I DON'T WANT TO HAVE TO DO THE WORK
IT WILL TAKE TO GET BETTER.

BUT IF I DON'T . . .   GOD, IF I DON'T . . .

IS THIS JUST WHAT LIFE IS NOW?

IS THIS WHAT IT'S GOING TO BE LIKE FOREVER?

small ghost goes grocery shopping pt. 2

She goes in for mangoes, paper towels, and white rice.

Starts feeling self-conscious
hovering around the blueberries
because what if someone is staring at her?
Because isn't someone always staring at her?

She can't remember why
she's trying to take care of herself,
so instead she buys Funfetti cake mix,
popcorn, and frozen pizza.

She tries to make eye contact with the checkout clerk,
but it's like he's looking right through her.

small ghost joins tiktok

Learns a dance or two,
shows no one;

forms an opinion or two,
tells no one;

tries to remember who she is,
but only ends up forgetting.

small ghost lurks on social media

Can't figure out how to break herself apart
into bite-sized
consumable
pieces
anymore.

Somebody's always choking on something.

What used to be a lifeline is now just a tightrope,
and she's too embarrassed to walk it,
even if no one
is looking.

She wants connection more than she wants to live,
maybe even more than she wants to die;

but it's too embarrassing to admit,
so she's choosing to wither away instead.

Looking around outside is enough
to make you want to give up.

Elaborate.

Haven't you seen the news?
I want to peel the skin off my face.
I don't want to exist in the kind of world
where these things are even possible.

And yet you do.

YOU WERE NOT MADE TO LIVE THIS WAY.

SOBBING OVER UNSENT TEXT MESSAGES

AND BINGE-WATCHING BAD TELEVISION.

SECOND JOBS AND MONETIZED HOBBIES.

SELF-MEDICATING WITH WHATEVER

MAKES YOU FORGET YOU'RE ALIVE.

This is pointless.
Therapy isn't going to fix me.
Friendship isn't going to fix me.
Religion isn't going to fix me.
Weed isn't going to fix me.
Wine isn't going to fix me.
Sobriety isn't going to fix me.
Poetry isn't going to fix me.
Moving isn't going to fix me.
Rest isn't going to fix me.
Love isn't going to fix me.
Medication isn't going to fix me—

Prove it.

Stay long enough
to say you tried everything.

Come share an orange with me.

exposed and vulnerable /
failing at simple tasks /
desperate for something
to dull the pain of living /
I'm tired of being lazy
and tragic / but every day
I have to wake up /
and make all these decisions
/ is anyone really living
the good life? / I'm not sure
I even know what it is /
I can't deal with my own head
/ how pathetic is that? /
medication feels like
giving up /

Doing nothing is giving up.

adjustment period

Not-quite-dead-tired for two weeks straight,
riding waves of nausea and regret
followed by panic attacks and headaches.
They tell me this is the price for a better life.
Set a timer for your medication
and wait three to six months
to see if you still want to kill yourself.

I don't want to talk about buzzwords,
but you need to take care of yourself.

Self-care? That's your answer?
Fuck you for making me feel like this
is my fault. Like I could buy enough
little treats for myself to fix my brain.
Like I could spend my money on
bath salts instead of therapy. Like if
I just sat outside for fifteen minutes and
exercised more I wouldn't be depressed.
I'm not sad. I'm depressed. If that shit
worked, nobody would be on Lexapro.

Why are you angry today?

I'm not angry.

Do you blame yourself?
For being this way?
For letting it get this far?
For not seeking help sooner?

SMALL GHOST NEEDS THE SAME TIRED ADVICE

EVERYONE GIVES

TO NOT ACTUALLY HELP HER.

SHE NEEDS THIS TO NOT BE HER FAULT.

SHE CANNOT HANDLE

ONE MORE THING

BEING HER FAULT.

Living is too draining. She insists she's not cut out for it.
It's too expensive.

Everything half-decent feels out of reach and

all time ever does is pass.

She's still trying to come to terms with it.

Sometimes she wonders if society was designed
to depress her / to make her worry / to make her lonely.

It's doing a good job.

Her only memories from last year are about working
and buying things.

small ghost turns up the volume when you're not looking

Anything to drown out the thoughts in her head.

She puts on a sad song.

And then she puts on another sad song.

And then she puts on another sad song
even though all it does is make her more sad.

And then she picks one sad song
to put on repeat for a week

until the words are meaningless
and all she's left with
is the feeling.

WEIRD BUT STILL CUTE

Small Ghost
@smallghostsighs

point me in the direction of the nearest void

2:55 AM · 10/6/15 From Earth

4 Reposts **4** Likes

small ghost downloads *sims 4*

Just to recreate her own house.
Just to make a miniature version of herself
that does
what it's supposed to do.

She takes care of the simulation
better than she does herself.

She keeps the ladders in the pool.
She never prays for house fires.

the years are pressing down on me like a stone /
love eludes me / joy is mythically scarce / I'm tired
of treading water / I tell you all the time / I've been
treating my own face like a jump scare

maybe I am the knife in the shower scene / but
I refuse to be the victim / and the killer, too

/ when I started writing about life / I didn't know
what it was like

and my mother says, *why do you have to
write about it? / can't you just keep some things
to yourself?* / and I say, / *no / I don't think I can*

poetry is a survival tactic
poetry is resistance
poetry is proof of existence

/ the things I could have done / the life I could
have lived / if I had been well / if I had been
safe / if I had been loved / there's no use
dwelling on it / misery has swallowed
enough of me / it has to be full

serious questions

Do I want to die, or do I need to eat?

Do I want to die, or do I need some fresh air?

Do I want to die, or do I need to sit in the sun?

Do I want to die, or am I getting my period in a week?

Do I want to die, or do I need more sleep?

Do I want to die, or do I need human interaction?

Do I want to die, or do I need a social media break?

Do I want to die, or am I feeling stuck and stagnant?

Do I want to die, or am I doomscrolling?

Do I want to die, or do I want a better world?

Do I want to die, or do I want my life to change?

And if I want to die:

can I at least procrastinate,

put it off for a year,

reevaluate at a later date?

What is it actually going to take
to bring you back to life?
I don't know.
I don't know.
But you'll rarely find it
sitting alone in your bedroom.

Eyes aching,   fingers trembling at the door.

You used to be someone. Maybe a long time ago. Maybe in a dream.

Now you're something else,   something tired and raw

weeping   wailing

   begging   but you   can't remember what for.

It's not always going to be like this. Take   the pills with food and water.

Wait for the fever to break,   wait for the light to come in.

It's gonna.

Wake up,   dead girl,

desire-driven and unremorseful.

It's time to start living again.

Come on,   Lazarus,   it's not over yet.

sorry to say it / I am nothing if not contradictory / but sometimes you do need to hide away in bed for a while / collecting tears in a jar and acting like a strange little creature / overeating and avoiding the light and indulging in your vices / be patient with yourself / you can't force recovery / spending energy you don't have is just going to send you spiraling back into hell / you do not deserve to be tortured in the pit just because you are alive /

when you are ready to return / your life will be waiting

small ghost has a new affirmation

you belong here

you belong here

you belong here

you belong here

you belong here

you belong here

you belong here

you belong here

you belong here

you belong here

you belong here

you belong here

small ghost makes a friend

He's a mess (just like her).
He always comes when he's called.
He hogs the bed, but she doesn't mind.
(She doesn't do a lot of sleeping anymore anyway.)

It's still nice to lie down with something warm.
It's still nice to hear the heart beat.

small ghost doesn't feel good

But also doesn't choke on the word *fine* anymore;
she's not sure if this is progress or acceptance.

All she knows
is that she's tired
of letting the things she doesn't forgive herself for
pile up like leaves in autumn.

You know,
it gets to a point where you can rake and rake and rake,
but the leaves just keep coming down
and children just keep making games
out of running through them.

It's so easy to feel trampled by absolutely nothing.

small ghost goes grocery shopping pt. 3

Wears headphones.
Makes eye contact with no one.

Bases her purchases on how bright the colors are,
how cute the packaging is.

Considers weeping at checkout (but doesn't).

Returns home to bake a cake and eats a slice alone
at the kitchen table,
even though what she wants to do
is carry the whole thing into her bedroom
and eat it with her hands
in the dark.

She feels like a feral cat trapped indoors
and a lamp with the bulb missing
and a girl who has forgotten
how to pass the time alone and sober.

poem ideas ♥ ♥ ♥

I'm just going to write down how I'm
feeling and hope it helps. If it
doesn't make sense, it doesn't
make sense. Fine. No one else
is ever going to read this
anyway. And look— it's not that
I believe we're all doomed and
life is going to suck forever.
But what if it does? And what
if we are? — and what if we're not?
I don't even know what I want my
life to look like. I don't even know
what I want. It's scary to want
things. I don't know if this is helping

I'm fine, I'm just thinking about fruit and original sin / Sylvia Plath and her writing routine / Aphrodite and Medusa / the myth of permanence / the weight of art / patterns from the past and what they mean for the future / I don't remember the last conversation I had with my first love / I doubt my father ever got sober but I have no way to ask him / I wish I could leave my physical form behind / before this body I was nothing but salt and light / I need to get a real job / I'll never have another Saturday morning eating cereal and watching cartoons with my little brother / he's not even little anymore / how is that fair? / he wasn't supposed to leave me behind / I bet I could create a sixth stage of grief just for me / I'm sorry / you know how it goes / you know what I am / I'm running on caffeine and maladaptive daydreams / do you think people miss me? / I can't tell if I've made an impact / or just a mess

There is a period of time after resurfacing
when the sight of your ruined life
might make you want to dive right back into the water
and follow that siren song all the way down—

(all those wasted months)   (all that squandered time)

but you haven't ruined your life.
You have saved it.
You're saving it right now.

when i want to die, instead

I go for a walk or

I take a cold shower or

I lie down on the kitchen floor
and pull the cat onto my chest or

I pick something new to learn about or

I make a list of food I want to eat
and hang it on the wall or

I do something that made me happy as a kid or

I make bad art on purpose or

I write weird poems in the notes app or

I fill my calendar with a million little things
to look forward to or

I change something about my life
even if it's just as small
as getting bangs.

apology tour

hey / me again / sorry for
disappearing / I was trapped
in a nightmare / I hope you
forgive me / I forgot how to
be human for a while / and
now I'm remembering

small ghost doesn't always have bad days

Doesn't always wake up feeling like she's six feet under,
doesn't always move through life like she's underwater,
doesn't always have to remind herself to smile,
doesn't always feel crushed
under the weight of something
nobody around her attempts to understand.

Sometimes she gets out of bed without forcing herself,
sometimes she remembers to eat regular meals,
sometimes she takes her vitamins,
   pays her bills,
   posts on Instagram,
   does the laundry.

Sometimes when she takes photos with friends,
it's not to prove to her mother that she's okay.

It's just because she wanted to savor a moment.

recovery is forever

Some burdens cannot be lifted
and instead
must be embraced and endured.

I only know one sure way
to ease this weight:

unravel what you're feeling

and speak the truth about it.

Bare your teeth and
bite back at that cruel voice in your head
trying to convince you this life is not worth living.

Tell it,

> *I am not done yet.*
> *I belong here.*
> *Your plan for my destruction*
> *will have to wait.*

One day you're going to look up
and realize
this is your life, outlaw.
These are the roads
you chose to run down.
This is the bet you made with God,
and now you ought to see it through.
Remember what the wind
felt like on your face?
Remember back when you held
the red beating heart
of possibility in your hands?
When you lived on honeysuckle
and sweet everythings?
Don't you miss the taste?
As long as you are alive,
there's time to sink your teeth into life
and suck it dry.
There's still flavor left in here.
There's still something to savor.

I AM A LOVER.

YOU WILL NEVER FIND ME NOT YEARNING.

I'M YEARNING RIGHT NOW.

WHAT DO YOU THINK A POEM IS?

life is unpredictable / by which I mean /
unclench your jaw / despite the odds /
tomorrow might actually be better /

Maybe we put too much pressure
on what it's supposed to be.
Maybe life is just a long conversation
between old friends,
and it doesn't have to mean something
or be any more complicated than that.

forgive yourself for being human / return
to your roots / eat some fruit in the sun /
try out uncomplicated joy / maybe it will
save you / otherwise maybe Sertraline /
Prozac / Effexor / come on, loser; get in,
we're going to therapy / if you're sick of
casting crying spells try out self-love potions
/ there's no shame in making it up as you go
/ everyone is doing it / whatever keeps you
alive is helping / I think if you're very lucky
/ maybe one day you won't have to survive
anymore / and you'll just be able to live

small ghost stands in a sunlit kitchen

In a relatively clean apartment, music on
and something sweet in the oven.

That's it.

And today, she lets it be enough.

It's true: hope
alone
will not fix the world.
But neither will despair.
Our lives are created
and destroyed by
action.

You can't wait
for everything
to be perfect
before you start
living your life.

You'll wait
forever.

Open your mind and lead with love.
Believe in the world you're dreaming of.
Treat each small delight like it lights up your life.
Live like it thrills you.

Keep hope alive until the moment it kills you.

That's all you can do.

the light pouring in from the window
looks like art on the wall / don't
get me wrong /
I'm still sad /
but sometimes I get caught up
in a tiny moment of beauty

/ and I think /

this is it / this is what they mean
when they talk about life

Go. Go on and

rage against time / against human error / against despair.

When you tire of bashing yourself
against the rocks /

                    I will meet you on the shore.

FEEL EVERYTHING.

EVERYTHING.

BUT YOU CAN'T
GET STUCK
IN IT.

With time, grief becomes   something else—

more like a flower you tend to
and less like

                              a hole
                               you
                               fall
                               into.

With time, you learn to
welcome the remembering

instead of

shrinking   away.

there's a big possibility
things will get worse
over the next few years
/ sit with that for a minute /
feel the soft edges of panic
fluttering in your chest
/ take a long look down
into the well of fear /
it's dark down there /
it's okay to acknowledge that

/ *real vibes only* /

look toward the bleakest future
and feel whatever you're feeling

/ now breathe /   /

Getting better
isn't about moving yourself
to a perpetual state
of joy and goodness and happiness.
It's about learning how to pick yourself up
and keep going, despite.
It's about betting there will be easier years than this one
and then sticking around long enough
to prove yourself right.

RESIST BITTERNESS, CALLOUSNESS, APATHY.

YOU WANT TO DISAPPEAR AGAIN,

BUT YOU CAN'T.

YOU HAVE TO FIGHT THIS TIME.

Wanting to be alive
is exhausting.

Oh, it's terrible.
Terrible and beautiful.
Open your door and
remember how it's done.

and I said,

why are all the poets so hopeful?

and she said,

because they've lived.

small ghost looks to the future

she thinks about flowers on her kitchen table
and the way light looks slipping through the
blinds at 10 a.m. /

she thinks about the taste of strawberries and other
people's mouths fresh with toothpaste / thinks about
airports and train stations and how rain makes everybody
feel a different way / thinks about bookshelves and frost
and instrumental movie soundtracks /

she thinks about how sweet it might feel to be soft again
/ thinks about thawing like ice / thinks about budding
like spring / thinks about laughing until it doesn't hurt to
breathe anymore /

she thinks about how hard it is to admit that she wants
things because it means she might not get them /

then she wants things anyway

i am

Despite all of it:
the months of barely breathing,
the hellfire and the hate,
the churning and the yearning and the agony—

I am still grateful to be here
on this weird spinning rock with the rest of you.

Eating pasta,
laughing with my friends,
making art,
chasing my daydreams,
drinking fresh orange crushes on the beach,
catching another sunrise,
listening to my heart,
and attempting to live.

dear reader,

It will not always feel like this—
and when it does feel like this,
you will learn to bear it
despite your tender heart
and your sore shoulders.
I promise it's worth it to stay.
You will not always be the ghost
haunting your own life.
I believe in you.

it seems dangerous

to be so

hopeful

but

I can't

resist

acknowledgments

Small Ghost is based on my 2015 chapbook of the same name.

To be honest, I never expected that little project would get the amount of love that it did. For something that was handmade and stapled together in my living room nearly ten years ago to turn into one of the most beloved, recommended, and sought-after pieces of my work—it's almost unthinkable to me.

Most of those original poems appear here, as well as some of the other random *Small Ghost*–style poems that have popped up in my work over the years.

This full-length book would never have been made if people weren't still asking for it.

All I can say is thank you.

Thank you to everyone behind the scenes who had a hand in working on this collection! Beau Adler, Natalie Noland, Jessica Peirce, Caitlyn Siehl, Molly Ringle, Michelle Halket and the team at Central Avenue. Nikita in general. My readers. My partners in crime. The poets and the poets-at-heart I consider my family. Thank you and thank you again for good measure.

I truly have to thank everyone who used to follow me on

Tumblr because they are the reason this book even exists. Super extra thank you to everyone who's stuck around from those days.

And a huge thank you to Lauren Zaknoun, who not only did the cover and the stunning interior ghost photography in this book—but she also did the cover and interior illustrations in the original chapbook back in 2015. Thank you for helping me bring this little story to light, Lauren.

Also shout-out to Zoloft.

Trista Mateer is a passionate mental health advocate, utilizing her large online platform (and her work) to destigmatize and springboard conversations surrounding grief, loss, trauma, anxiety, depression, etc. A multifaceted creative force, Mateer is best known for *Aphrodite Made Me Do It*—a collection of art and poetry—which explores modern feminist issues through the lens of Greek mythology. Whatever she's writing about, Mateer invites readers into a world where vulnerability is celebrated.

Connect with her on Instagram and TikTok @tristamateer or at tristamateer.com

Lauren Zaknoun is a Lebanese-American photographer and visual artist. Her work reflects the human condition, the universal desire to be seen and known. Anxiety, absence, escapism, and humor are recurring themes in her work. Based in southeastern New England, Lauren can be found photographing the local cranberry bogs, concerts, and her cat, Phoebe. Connect with her at @laurenzaknounart or at zaknoun.co

Also by Trista Mateer

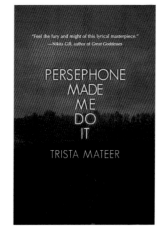

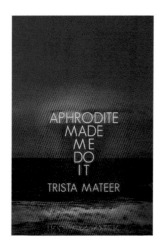